GRAPHIC DISCOVERIES
ANCIENT TREASURES

by Rob Shone

illustrated by Nick Spender

Rosen Classroom Books & Materials ™
New York

Published in 2008 by The Rosen Publishing Group, Inc.
29 East 21st Street, New York, NY 10010

Designed and produced by
David West Books

Editor: Gail Bushnell

Photo credits:
44t, USGS; 44mr, Marco Regalia; 44b, Maria Reiche; 44bl, Matija Podhraiki; 45tl, Tomasz Resiak; 45tr, Arjen Briene; 45mr, Emile Gsell; 45bl, Les Byerley; 45br, Matthew Scherf.

Library of Congress Cataloging-in-Publication Data

Shone, Rob.
  Ancient treasures / by Rob Shone ; illustrated by Nick Spender. -- 1st ed.
     p. cm. -- (Graphic discoveries).
  Includes bibliographical references and index.
  ISBN-13: 978-1-4042-1089-9 (library binding)
  ISBN-13: 978-1-4042-9594-0 (6 pack)
  ISBN-13: 978-1-4042-9593-3 (pbk.)
  1. Antiquities--Juvenile literature. 2. Excavations (Archaeology)--Juvenile literature.
  3. Archaeology--Juvenile literature. 4. Civilization, Ancient--Juvenile literature. I.
  Spender, Nick. II. Title.
  CC171.S55 2007
  930.1--dc22

                                     2007004750

Manufactured in China

CONTENTS

HUNTING FOR TREASURES

Today, hunting for treasures has become a science—archaeology. It is the study of our past through exploration, excavation, and analysis of places and items uncovered.

EARLY DAYS

The earliest treasure hunters were the tomb raiders of ancient Egypt. Most tombs of the pharaohs were broken into by thieves, searching for gold and precious jewelry. Many ancient sites have been damaged by careless digging and excavation by some 19th-century archaeologists. These treasure hunters were more interested in collecting precious items for their value, rather than their historical importance.

MODERN ARCHAEOLOGY

Searching for historical sites has become more exact. Technology plays a big part, although accidental finds and amateurs still provide surprising results. Recently, the true location of the island of Ithaca may have been found by an amateur. The island was the home of the hero Odysseus, whose epic journey from the Trojan War is told in Homer's *Odyssey*.

1. Aerial photographs can reveal surprising details of buildings that cannot be seen from the ground. The markings in the field (a) show evidence of an early settlement.

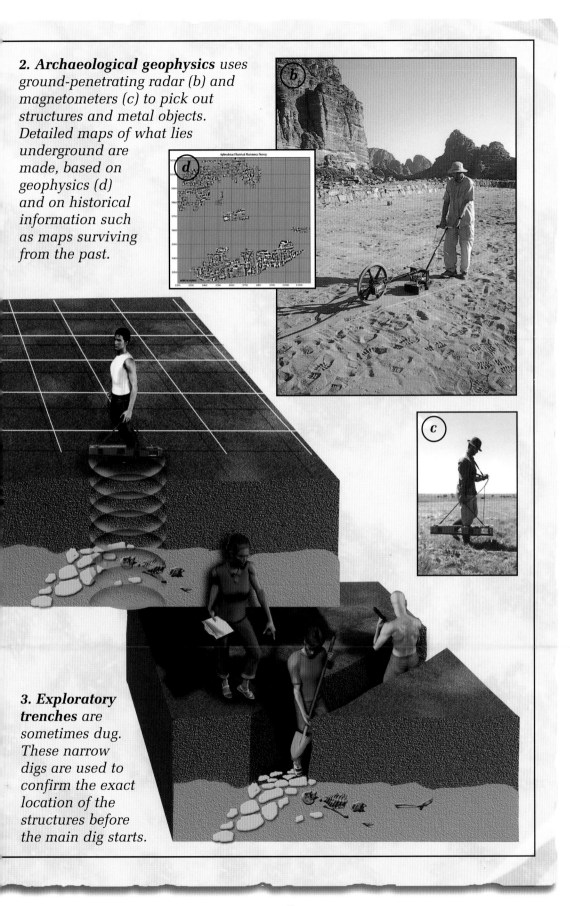

2. Archaeological geophysics uses ground-penetrating radar (b) and magnetometers (c) to pick out structures and metal objects. Detailed maps of what lies underground are made, based on geophysics (d) and on historical information such as maps surviving from the past.

Aphrodisias Electrical Resistance Survey

3. Exploratory trenches are sometimes dug. These narrow digs are used to confirm the exact location of the structures before the main dig starts.

DIGGING UP THE PAST

Once the archaeological site has been mapped, it is ready to be dug up. This requires painstaking work. Teams of diggers scrape away the earth, layer after layer. It is during this stage that lost coins, fragments of pottery, and human bones are discovered. Occasionally, an amazing piece of jewelry is found, which may have been lost hundreds of years ago.

Archaeological digs often have to work around immovable objects, like this gas pipe next to a Roman horse burial (above).

EXCAVATION

A grid of white string covers the site. This allows for detailed cataloging of all artifacts found. Each digger has to note the position of the find before it is removed. Even the earth removed from the digging is put through screens to collect any small pieces that may have been missed. Very gradually, the site is revealed.

ANALYSIS

Excavation is only part of the work. After excavation, the job of cleaning, analyzing, and interpreting begins. After cleaning, some pieces may need to be treated to preserve them. After they are labeled, they are sent to be analyzed. This can include carbon dating and X-raying, as well as experts looking at them in detail. Often, several pieces from one object are stuck back together. Eventually, well-preserved objects find their way into museums.

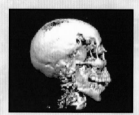

CAT scans (above) and X-rays are used to explore the insides of artifacts. This is useful for seeing inside encrusted items from shipwrecks and mummies. In 2005, the first CAT scan of Tutankhamen solved the riddle of his death. It looks as if he died from blood poisoning, caused by a broken leg.

The earth is put into a bucket, which is then taken to screens.

A digger uses a simple triangular trowel to scrape away the earth a bit at a time.

Finds, such as human remains, are marked on a map, and notes are made before removal.

A brush and a dentist's probe are used for detailed work.

A skull is cleaned before it is labeled and bagged.

Using computer programs, people's heads can be reconstructed from skulls, to see what they looked like.

THE HUNT FOR TROY

THE STORY OF TROY AND THE TROJAN WAR BEGAN IN SPARTA, GREECE. PARIS, SON OF PRIAM, KING OF TROY, HAD BEEN SENT THERE AS AN AMBASSADOR TO THE COURT OF KING MENELAUS.

MENELAUS HAD A BEAUTIFUL WIFE NAMED HELEN. PARIS FELL IN LOVE THE MOMENT HE SAW HER.

PARIS PERSUADED HELEN TO LEAVE SPARTA AND SAIL TO TROY WITH HIM.

MENELAUS WAS FURIOUS. HE WENT TO SEE HIS BROTHER AGAMEMNON, KING OF MYCENAE.

EVERY KING IN GREECE WILL SUPPORT YOU, MENELAUS. WE WILL TAKE AN ARMY TO TROY AND BRING HER BACK.

A THOUSAND SHIPS CARRIED THE GREEK ARMY ACROSS THE SEA TO TROY.

THE CITY OF TROY WAS RICH AND POWERFUL, AND ITS WALLS WERE TALL AND STRONG. HELEN WOULD NOT LEAVE PARIS, AND THE GREEKS COULD NOT TAKE THE CITY BY FORCE. ALL THEY COULD DO WAS LAY A SIEGE AND STARVE THE CITY INTO SURRENDERING.

THE TROJANS WERE FIERCE FIGHTERS, THOUGH. AGAIN AND AGAIN THEY LEFT THE CITY AND DROVE OFF THE GREEKS.

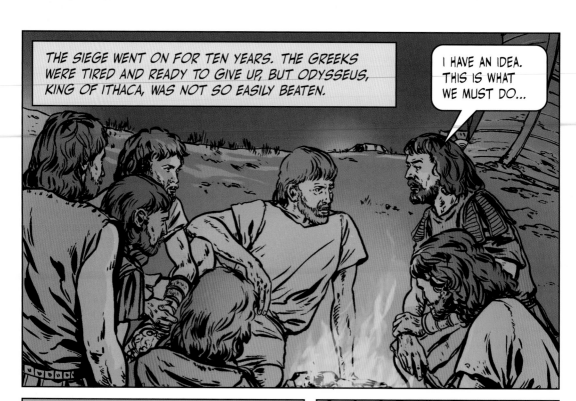

THE SIEGE WENT ON FOR TEN YEARS. THE GREEKS WERE TIRED AND READY TO GIVE UP, BUT ODYSSEUS, KING OF ITHACA, WAS NOT SO EASILY BEATEN.

I HAVE AN IDEA. THIS IS WHAT WE MUST DO...

EVERY DAY FOR TEN YEARS THE TROJANS HAD WOKEN TO THE SIGHT OF THE GREEK ARMY SURROUNDING THEIR WALLS. THEN ONE MORNING IT WAS GONE. IN ITS PLACE STOOD A HUGE WOODEN HORSE.

A GREEK DESERTER STOOD NEXT TO IT.

THEY'VE GONE BACK TO GREECE. THEY LEFT THIS AS A GIFT FOR YOU.

THE TROJANS, OVERJOYED THAT THE LONG WAR WAS OVER, DRAGGED THE STATUE INTO THE CITY.

THEY CELEBRATED ALL DAY AND NIGHT.

THE GREEKS HAD NOT SAILED FOR HOME, AND THE HORSE WAS NOT WHAT IT SEEMED TO BE. WHILE THE TROJANS WERE ASLEEP...

GREEK SOLDIERS HAD BEEN HIDING INSIDE THE HORSE.

THEY OPENED THE CITY GATES AND SIGNALED TO THE REST OF THE GREEK ARMY.

THE GREEKS RUSHED INTO THE CITY.

THE TROJANS WERE UNPREPARED. THOSE WHO WERE NOT KILLED WERE MADE INTO SLAVES. ONLY A FEW MANAGED TO ESCAPE.

KING PRIAM AND PARIS WERE KILLED, AND THE CITY WAS BURNED TO THE GROUND. HELEN WAS TAKEN BACK TO SPARTA.

MANY STORIES WERE WRITTEN AND TOLD ABOUT THE WAR. THE MOST FAMOUS WAS THE EPIC POEM THE ILIAD. THE ANCIENT GREEKS BELIEVED THE ILIAD WAS A TRUE HISTORY. BY THE 19TH CENTURY, MOST SCHOLARS THOUGHT THAT TROY AND THE WAR WERE A MYTH. A FEW DISAGREED, AND THOUGHT THAT TROY WAS AT A PLACE CALLED BUNARBASHI IN ANATOLIA, WESTERN TURKEY.

IT WAS 1886, AND HEINRICH SCHLIEMANN HAD SPENT TWO DAYS AT BUNARBASHI, SEARCHING FOR TROY. SCHLIEMANN WAS A RICH GERMAN BUSINESSMAN. AT 44 YEARS OLD, HE HAD GIVEN UP HIS BUSINESS TO BECOME AN ARCHAEOLOGIST.

NOTHING! NOT EVEN A PIECE OF BROKEN POTTERY!

SCHLIEMANN WAS ABOUT TO LEAVE TURKEY WHEN HE MET FRANK CALVERT, AN ENGLISH DIPLOMAT AND AMATEUR ARCHAEOLOGIST.

I HEAR THAT YOU'VE BEEN DIGGING AT BUNARBASHI, SCHLIEMANN. YOU WON'T FIND TROY THERE.

WHAT MAKES YOU SAY THAT, CALVERT?

BECAUSE I KNOW WHERE TROY IS.

A FEW DAYS LATER, FRANK CALVERT AND HEINRICH SCHLIEMANN WERE STANDING ON A SMALL HILL CALLED HISSARLIK, 5 MILES (8 KM) FROM BUNARBASHI.

IT ALL FITS, SCHLIEMANN. THE RIVERS, THE BAY, THE SPRINGS—EVERYTHING. IT'S JUST AS IT'S DESCRIBED HERE IN THE ILIAD. THIS **HAS** TO BE TROY!

YOU SAID YOU HAD SOMETHING TO SHOW ME.

THERE—IT'S A TEMPLE. I'VE BEEN EXCAVATING THE HILL FOR YEARS. I OWN THIS EASTERN HALF.

THE THING IS, SCHLIEMANN, I DON'T HAVE THE MONEY TO KEEP DIGGING. I'VE TRIED TO GET THE BRITISH MUSEUM TO PAY FOR MORE WORK ON THE SITE, BUT THEY'RE NOT INTERESTED. I WAS THINKING MAYBE YOU COULD HELP.

CALVERT, IF YOU ARE RIGHT AND THIS IS TROY, WE SHALL BE FAMOUS!

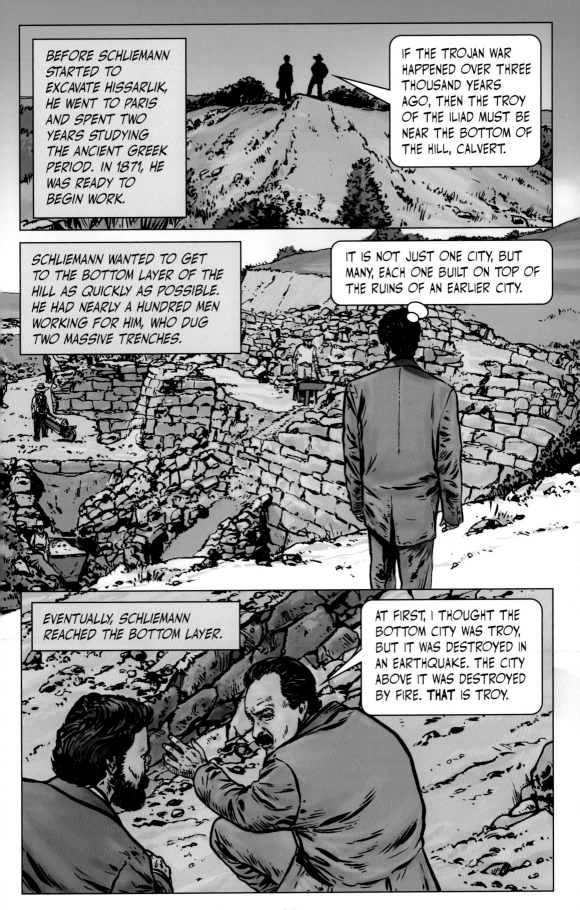

BEFORE SCHLIEMANN STARTED TO EXCAVATE HISSARLIK, HE WENT TO PARIS AND SPENT TWO YEARS STUDYING THE ANCIENT GREEK PERIOD. IN 1871, HE WAS READY TO BEGIN WORK.

IF THE TROJAN WAR HAPPENED OVER THREE THOUSAND YEARS AGO, THEN THE TROY OF THE ILIAD MUST BE NEAR THE BOTTOM OF THE HILL, CALVERT.

SCHLIEMANN WANTED TO GET TO THE BOTTOM LAYER OF THE HILL AS QUICKLY AS POSSIBLE. HE HAD NEARLY A HUNDRED MEN WORKING FOR HIM, WHO DUG TWO MASSIVE TRENCHES.

IT IS NOT JUST ONE CITY, BUT MANY, EACH ONE BUILT ON TOP OF THE RUINS OF AN EARLIER CITY.

EVENTUALLY, SCHLIEMANN REACHED THE BOTTOM LAYER.

AT FIRST, I THOUGHT THE BOTTOM CITY WAS TROY, BUT IT WAS DESTROYED IN AN EARTHQUAKE. THE CITY ABOVE IT WAS DESTROYED BY FIRE. **THAT** IS TROY.

SCHLIEMANN TOOK THE OBJECTS TO CALVERT'S HOUSE.

SEE, CALVERT! I WAS RIGHT. IT **MUST** BE TROY. HERE IS THE PROOF! I WILL CALL IT "KING PRIAM'S TREASURE."

IN 1874, SCHLIEMANN ANNOUNCED HIS DISCOVERY TO THE WORLD. HIS WIFE, SOPHIA, WAS PHOTOGRAPHED WEARING A GOLD HEADDRESS. HE CALLED IT THE "JEWELS OF HELEN."

SCHLIEMANN AND CALVERT SMUGGLED THE TREASURE OUT OF TURKEY. IT CAUSED A SENSATION. A MYTHICAL PLACE APPEARED TO BE REAL. SCHLIEMANN TOOK ALL THE CREDIT AND DID NOT MENTION CALVERT'S PART IN THE DISCOVERY. IT IS NOW KNOWN THAT SCHLIEMANN'S TROY AND TREASURE ARE 1,000 YEARS TOO EARLY TO BE THE TROY OF THE ILIAD. TODAY, HOWEVER, MOST ARCHAEOLOGISTS THINK THAT HISSARLIK IS INDEED WHERE TROY LIES.

THE END

TUTANKHAMEN'S TOMB

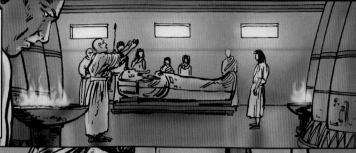

SPRING 1324 B.C., THE GREAT TEMPLE OF AMON AT KARNAK, EGYPT. NEARLY TEN WEEKS HAD PASSED SINCE THE YOUNG KING'S SUDDEN DEATH.

HE WAS ONLY 18 WHEN HE DIED, AND HAD REIGNED FOR NINE YEARS.

HIS YOUNG WIFE, ANKHESENAMEN, LAID A BUNCH OF WILDFLOWERS ON THE COFFIN.

THE PHARAOH'S BODY WAS CARRIED FROM THE TEMPLE IN A SHRINE SHAPED LIKE A BOAT.

THE GOLDEN COFFIN WAS TAKEN ACROSS THE RIVER NILE...

...AND TO THE VALLEY OF THE KINGS. FOR 1,000 YEARS THE PHARAOHS OF EGYPT HAD BEEN BURIED THERE.

THE COFFIN WAS PLACED IN A TOMB CARVED OUT OF THE ROCK. IN TIME, THE PEOPLE OF EGYPT FORGOT ALL ABOUT THE YOUNG KING.

SPRING 1922, HIGHCLERE CASTLE, ENGLAND. ARCHAEOLOGIST HOWARD CARTER HAD BEEN A VISITOR TO LORD CARNARVON'S HOME MANY TIMES. THE TWO MEN SHARED A PASSION FOR ANCIENT EGYPT.

LORD CARNARVON USED HIS WEALTH TO PAY FOR CARTER'S EXCAVATIONS. IN RETURN, MANY OF THE ARTIFACTS UNEARTHED BY CARTER FOUND THEIR WAY INTO CARNARVON'S COLLECTION AT HIGHCLERE.

SINCE 1917, CARTER HAD BEEN DIGGING IN THE VALLEY OF THE KINGS, AT LUXOR, IN EGYPT. HE WAS SURE THAT THE TOMB OF THE PHARAOH TUTANKHAMEN WAS THERE—UNTOUCHED.

LORD CARNARVON. I'VE BROUGHT THE PLANS FOR THIS SEASON'S EXCAVATIONS. I'D LIKE TO GO OVER THEM WITH YOU.

WE'VE SPENT FIVE YEARS DIGGING IN THE VALLEY, AND FOUND NOTHING.

CARTER, I'VE BEEN THINKING ABOUT THAT. LET'S GO TO THE LIBRARY.

IT'S COST ME A SMALL FORTUNE, AND I HAVE VERY LITTLE TO SHOW FOR IT.

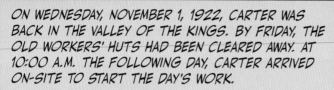

ON WEDNESDAY, NOVEMBER 1, 1922, CARTER WAS BACK IN THE VALLEY OF THE KINGS. BY FRIDAY, THE OLD WORKERS' HUTS HAD BEEN CLEARED AWAY. AT 10:00 A.M. THE FOLLOWING DAY, CARTER ARRIVED ON-SITE TO START THE DAY'S WORK.

IT WAS A RULE THAT IF ANYTHING WAS FOUND, THE WORKERS STOPPED DIGGING.

MR. CARTER, SIR! OVER HERE!

THE MEN HAVE STOPPED WORKING. THEY'VE FOUND SOMETHING!

A STEP CARVED OUT OF THE ROCK!

TWELVE STEPS LED DOWN TO A PLASTER WALL, AND BEYOND THAT, A RUBBLE-FILLED PASSAGEWAY. AS SOON AS HE HEARD THE NEWS, LORD CARNARVON RUSHED FROM ENGLAND TO JOIN CARTER.

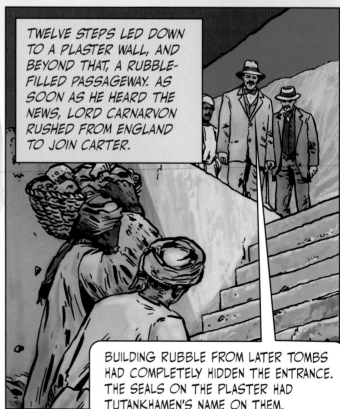

BUILDING RUBBLE FROM LATER TOMBS HAD COMPLETELY HIDDEN THE ENTRANCE. THE SEALS ON THE PLASTER HAD TUTANKHAMEN'S NAME ON THEM.

ON DECEMBER 18, CARTER INVITED PROFESSOR JAMES BREASTED TO THE SITE. BREASTED WAS AN EXPERT IN EGYPTIAN SEALS.

WE BROKE INTO THE TOMB THE FOLLOWING DAY, THE 27TH. I HAD THIS WALL BUILT TO GUARD AGAINST FLOODING.

I DON'T RECOGNIZE SOME OF THE ROYAL SEALS.

I WAS HOPING YOU COULD HELP IDENTIFY THEM FOR US, BREASTED.

WE CALL THIS ROOM THE ANTECHAMBER. IT'S JUST THE WAY WE FOUND IT. NOTHING HAS BEEN MOVED.

CARTER...

...IT'S LIKE SOMETHING FROM A FAIRY TALE!

YOU CAN SEE THERE ARE TWO PLASTERED DOORWAYS LEADING TO OTHER ROOMS. WE'VE NAMED THAT ONE THE ANNEX. IT'S PACKED FROM FLOOR TO CEILING WITH FURNITURE.

THAT'S WHERE ROBBERS BROKE INTO IT. THEY LEFT THE ROOM A MESS.

IF TUTANKHAMEN'S BODY IS HERE, IT LIES BEHIND THAT DOOR—IN THE TOMB CHAMBER.

CARTER SPENT THE NEXT THREE MONTHS WORKING IN THE ANTECHAMBER AND ANNEX.

BEFORE ANY OBJECT WAS MOVED, IT WAS GIVEN A NUMBER AND PHOTOGRAPHED.

EACH PIECE WAS THEN CAREFULLY WRAPPED...

...AND STORED IN THE NEARBY EMPTY TOMB OF AKHENATEN BEFORE BEING TAKEN TO CAIRO MUSEUM.

BESIDES WORKING IN THE TOMB, CARTER HAD TO DEAL WITH A STREAM OF GUESTS AND VISITORS.

THESE WOODEN BOXES HOLD FOOD FOR THE KING TO EAT IN THE NEXT LIFE.

THE ROOMS CONTAIN MANY OF TUTANKHAMEN'S PERSONAL THINGS. THIS IS ONE OF HIS CHARIOTS. YOU CAN SEE THAT THE WHEELS ARE WORN. HE MUST HAVE USED IT WHEN HE WAS ALIVE.

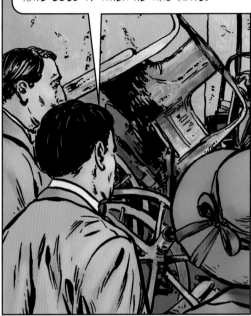

AND THIS IS TUTANKHAMEN'S THRONE. IT SHOWS THE KING AND HIS WIFE, ANKHESENAMEN.

ON FEBRUARY 16, IN FRONT OF EGYPTIAN OFFICIALS AND FELLOW ARCHAEOLOGISTS, CARTER BEGAN THE WORK OF BREAKING INTO THE TOMB CHAMBER ITSELF.

CARTER CAREFULLY CHIPPED AWAY THE PLASTER DOOR...

...TO REVEAL...

...A WALL OF GOLD. IT WAS A SHRINE.

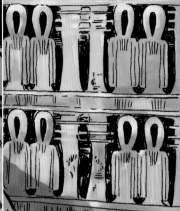

THE WOODEN SHRINE COVERED IN GOLD ALMOST FILLED THE TOMB CHAMBER.

HOW DID THEY GET IT INTO SUCH A SMALL SPACE?

IT WAS MADE ELSEWHERE, TAKEN APART, AND REBUILT IN HERE.

AT ONE END OF THE SHRINE WAS A PAIR OF DOORS.

I'M GOING TO UNDO THE BOLTS.

INSIDE THAT WAS ANOTHER COFFIN. LIKE THE FIRST, IT HAD BEEN WRAPPED IN CLOTH THAT HAD BECOME BLACK AND WORN WITH AGE. BOTH COFFINS WERE MADE OF WOOD, COVERED WITH A THIN LAYER OF GOLD.

THAT'S UNUSUAL. THERE'S A BUNCH OF FLOWERS ON THE FOREHEAD. I WONDER WHO PUT IT THERE?

INSIDE THAT COFFIN WAS A THIRD. IT, TOO, WAS WRAPPED IN TATTERED CLOTH. BUT THIS ONE WAS DIFFERENT FROM THE OTHERS. WHEN CARTER HAD CLEANED IT...

IT'S MADE OF **SOLID GOLD**, ARTHUR!

ON OCTOBER 28, 1925, THE LID OF THE GOLD COFFIN WAS RAISED. BENEATH IT LAY THE BODY OF TUTANKHAMEN. THE MUMMY WAS IN POOR CONDITION.

THE PRIESTS USED TOO MUCH PURIFYING RESIN. IT'S HARDENED AND GLUED EVERYTHING TOGETHER.

ON THE BODY WERE BRACELETS AND RINGS, AND HIDDEN IN THE BANDAGES WERE DOZENS OF SACRED CHARMS. IT TOOK HOURS OF WORK TO FREE THE FUNERAL MASK FROM THE BODY. CARTER HAD TO MELT THE HARDENED RESIN, USING HEATED KNIVES.

HE SEPARATED THE HEAD FROM THE REST OF THE MUMMY IN ORDER TO UNWRAP ITS BANDAGES. AFTER THREE YEARS OF WORK, CARTER FINALLY LOOKED UPON THE FACE OF THE PHARAOH TUTANKHAMEN.

A FINAL ROOM LED OFF FROM THE TOMB CHAMBER. CARTER CALLED IT THE TREASURY. ONCE THE COFFINS HAD BEEN TAKEN AWAY, CARTER COULD OPEN IT. INSIDE WAS A SMALL SHRINE THAT HOUSED THE KING'S INTERNAL ORGANS.

CARTER SPENT TEN YEARS WORKING ON THE TOMB. OVER 3,000 ITEMS WERE FOUND INSIDE IT. THE DISCOVERY SPARKED A WORLDWIDE FASCINATION WITH ANCIENT EGYPT, WHICH STILL CONTINUES. TUTANKHAMEN'S BODY WAS RETURNED TO HIS TOMB.

THE END

31

THE TERRA-COTTA ARMY

MARCH 1974, CHINA. IT HAD BEEN A DRY WINTER IN SHAANXI PROVINCE, AND WATER LEVELS WERE LOW. THE FARMERS OF XIYANG VILLAGE WERE DIGGING A WELL TO WATER THEIR SPRING CROPS.

COME ON, YANG! PUT YOUR BACK INTO IT!

I'VE BEEN DOWN HERE FOR HOURS. IT MUST BE YOUR TURN NOW.

GIVE IT TEN MORE MINUTES.

HUH?

CLANK!

WHAT'S THAT YOU'VE FOUND?

I DON'T KNOW.

ARRGH!

YANG! WHAT'S WRONG?

IT'S A...IT'S A...

...IT'S A HEAD! A POTTERY HEAD!

LOOK, THERE'S MORE OVER HERE—A TORSO AND SOME RUSTY METAL!

WHAT SHOULD WE DO?

HELP ME GET IT ALL INTO THE WHEELBARROW. WE CAN SELL THE METAL FOR SCRAP, AND THE POTTERY WILL MAKE GOOD STORAGE JARS.

FOUR YEARS LATER, YUAN ZHONGYI WAS STILL EXCAVATING THE SITE. HE FOUND OVER 6,000 TERRA-COTTA CHINESE WARRIORS IN A PIT THE SIZE OF 25 FOOTBALL FIELDS. THE OUTSIDE WORLD HAD HEARD OF THE FIND AND WAS EAGER TO LEARN MORE ABOUT IT.

PROFESSOR, WHO WERE ALL THESE WARRIORS MADE FOR?

THERE ARE THREE OTHER PITS AS WELL, ALTHOUGH ONE IS EMPTY.

NOT ONLY ARE THERE INFANTRYMEN, WE HAVE ALSO FOUND ARCHERS, HORSES, AND CAVALRYMEN, CHARIOTS, AND EVEN THEIR COMMANDERS.

THE EMPEROR QIN* SHI HUANGDI. HIS TOMB IS A MILE FROM HERE.

*PRONOUNCED "CHIN."

HE LIVED OVER TWO THOUSAND YEARS AGO. CHINA TAKES ITS NAME FROM HIM, ALTHOUGH WHEN HE WAS BORN, IT WAS NOT A SINGLE COUNTRY...

AT THAT TIME, CHINA WAS MADE UP OF SEVEN KINGDOMS. THEY HAD BEEN AT WAR WITH EACH OTHER SINCE 475 B.C.

IN 247 B.C. 12-YEAR-OLD QIN SHI HUANGDI BECAME KING OF QIN, A KINGDOM IN THE FAR WEST OF CHINA. OVER THE NEXT 26 YEARS, THE ARMIES OF QIN CONQUERED THE OTHER SIX STATES.

IN 221 B.C., QIN SHI HUANGDI MADE HIMSELF THE FIRST EMPEROR OF A UNITED COUNTRY.

QIN SHI HUANGDI SET ABOUT REFORMING THE NEW COUNTRY. HE ORGANIZED A SINGLE SYSTEM OF WRITING THAT EVERYONE COULD READ AND UNDERSTAND. HE APPOINTED THOUSANDS OF OFFICIALS AND CLERKS TO HELP RUN THE COUNTRY.

TO KEEP THE COUNTRY SAFE FROM INVADERS, HE BUILT A WALL. IT WAS TO BECOME THE GREAT WALL OF CHINA. ALMOST A MILLION SLAVES AND PRISONERS WERE FORCED TO WORK ON IT. THOUSANDS DIED AND WERE BURIED INSIDE IT.

HE ALSO ORDERED A TOMB TO BE BUILT. IT WAS TO BE HIS HOME AFTER HIS DEATH...

...AND, TO KEEP HIM SAFE FROM ENEMIES IN THE AFTERLIFE, HE WOULD NEED AN ARMY.

THOUSANDS OF WORKERS AND CRAFTSMEN WERE USED TO CREATE AN ARMY MADE OUT OF CLAY.

FIRST THE BODIES OF THE FIGURES WERE MADE, USING THICK COILS OF CLAY.

THE HANDS AND HEADS WERE MADE SEPARATELY. EACH HEAD WAS MODELED ON A REAL SOLDIER. NO TWO HEADS WERE THE SAME.

THE ROUGH BODY WAS THEN COATED IN A LAYER OF FINE CLAY, AND DETAILS OF THE CLOTHING AND ARMOR ADDED.

THE POTTERY PIECES WERE THEN FIRED TO HARDEN THEM. A RAP WITH THE KNUCKLES TOLD THE POTTER IF THE FIGURES HAD FIRED PROPERLY.

DUNK!

KNOCK

PERFECT.

NEXT, THE HEADS AND HANDS WERE STUCK ONTO THE BODIES...

...AND THE FIGURES PAINTED.

FINALLY, THE FINISHED SOLDIERS WERE TAKEN TO THE PITS, PLACED IN POSITION, AND EACH GIVEN A WEAPON. A ROOF WAS BUILT OVER THE PIT AND COVERED WITH EARTH.

IN 210 B.C., QIN SHI HUANGDI DIED. HIS COFFIN WAS PLACED IN AN UNDERGROUND PALACE, BURIED DEEP BENEATH A PYRAMID OF EARTH 300 FEET (92 M) HIGH.

THE CEILING OF THE ROOM IN WHICH QIN SHI HUANGDI LAY WAS STUDDED WITH PEARLS, MARKING THE STARS AND CONSTELLATIONS. QIN'S COPPER COFFIN RESTED ON THE BACK OF A DRAGON.

THE FLOOR WAS A MAP OF QIN'S EMPIRE. MERCURY FLOWED DOWN EVERY RIVER AND INTO A MERCURY SEA. AROUND THE ROOM WERE CHESTS FULL OF GOLD, JEWELS, AND SILK.

THE EMPEROR WAS NOT ALONE. ALL THE WORKERS AND OFFICIALS WHO HAD BUILT THE UNDERGROUND PALACE, AND KNEW ITS SECRETS, WERE BURIED WITH HIM.

QIN SHI HUANGDI WAS SUCCEEDED BY HIS SON, HUHAI. HE WAS A WEAK EMPEROR, AND SOON THE COUNTRY WAS TORN BY CIVIL WAR.

THE REBELS RAIDED THE MAUSOLEUM.

TAKE THE WEAPONS, AND SET FIRE TO THE PLACE!

THE FIRES BURNED FOR THREE MONTHS.

CHINESE HISTORIANS WROTE THAT THE TOMB ITSELF WAS BROKEN INTO.

COME ON! DON'T WORRY ABOUT HIM!

WE WILL NOT ENTER THE TOMB UNTIL WE ARE SURE HOW TO PRESERVE WHAT WE FIND IN IT.

FOR NOW, WE ARE TRYING TO RESTORE AS MANY OF THE BROKEN FIGURES AS POSSIBLE. IT IS A SLOW JOB.

AH! A PIECE THAT FITS! IT'S THE FIRST ONE THIS WEEK.

THOUSANDS OF PEOPLE, FROM ALL AROUND THE WORLD, VISIT THE MUSEUM EACH YEAR. OTHER LIFE-SIZE TERRA-COTTA FIGURES HAVE BEEN FOUND, INCLUDING ACROBATS AND COURT OFFICIALS. THERE COULD BE MORE FINDS, JUST AS SPECTACULAR AS EMPEROR QIN'S ARMY, STILL WAITING TO BE DISCOVERED.

THE END

FAMOUS ANCIENT TREASURES

Ancient treasures dot the world, from Mayan temples in the Americas, to terra-cotta armies in China. As well as revealing fabulous gold objects, jewelry, and other artifacts, these sites offer a wealth of invaluable historical information.

ROSETTA STONE

One of the greatest finds was the Rosetta Stone. Discovered in 1799 by the French, it provided one of the major breakthroughs to understanding the ancient Egyptian language. Until then, ancient Egyptian picture words, called hieroglyphs, were a mystery. Written on the stone are Egyptian hieroglyphs and their translation in classical Greek. As scholars could read classical Greek, the hieroglyphs puzzle was soon solved.

The Rosetta Stone

White House Ruins
Ancient canyon dwellings of the Anasazi people.

Ancient Temples
Aztec and Maya people.

Ancient Calendar
Aztec people.

Sacrifice Knife
Inca people.

Nazca Monkey
Giant lines in the Nazca desert, Peru. Nazca people.

Stonehenge
Circle of standing stones from the Bronze Age.

Terra-cotta Warriors
See pages 32–43.

Agamemnon's Mask
Found by Schliemann in a Mycenean grave.

Angkor Wat
12th-century temple in Cambodia.

Priam's Treasure
See pages 8 to 17.

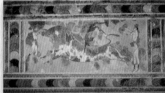

Knossos Palace
Fresco of bull-leaping.

Aboriginal Rock
Art of the Gagudju people of northern Australia.

Tutankhamen Head Mask
See pages 18–31.

GLOSSARY

aerial photograph A photograph taken from a balloon, aircraft, spacecraft, or satellite.

ambassador Someone chosen by a government to act for or represent it abroad.

analysis Detailed examination.

archaeology The study of our past through exploration, excavation, and analysis of places and items uncovered.

artifacts Items that have been dug up, which have been made by humans and that don't naturally occur in the ground.

carbon dating A way of measuring how old an item is, using a special machine that looks at the item's carbon atoms.

cataloging Making a detailed list and description.

clerk Someone in charge of keeping official records.

constellation A group of stars that often form a distinctive shape in the sky.

excavation The removal of earth by digging.

geophysics The study of the Earth. In archaeology it relates to the methods for exploring what is under the ground, using devices such as GPR and magnetometers.

ground penetrating radar (GPR) A device that uses radio waves that bounce off objects underground to create a map showing the objects' location.

interpreting To explain or understand the meaning of something.

magnetometer A device that locates metal objects underground.

mausoleum A large building containing a tomb.

pharaoh A ruler of ancient Egypt.

preserve To treat something so that it keeps its present condition.

radar A system for finding the position of distant objects. It transmits radio waves from an aerial and detects signals reflected back from an object in its path.

reconstruct To create a description or idea from the evidence available.

resin A sticky substance that comes from plants.

sarcophagus A coffin made of stone.

screens A horizontal frame with fine wire netting used to sift soil from a dig in order to find small objects.

seal A piece of wax or clay stamped with a name.

shrine A box or room that contains something of religious value.

siege The surrounding of a fortified place by an army.

torso The part of the body without the arms, legs, and head.

FOR MORE INFORMATION

ORGANIZATIONS

Peabody Museum of Archaeology and Ethnology
11 Divinity Avenue
Harvard University
Cambridge, MA 02138
(617) 496-1027
Web site: http://www.peabody.harvard.edu/

American Museum of Natural History
Central Park West at 79th Street
New York, NY 10024-5192
(212) 769-5100
Web site: http://www.amnh.org/

FURTHER READING

Barnes, Trevor. *Archaeology*. Boston, MA: Kingfisher, 2004.

Devereux, Paul. *Archaeology: The Study of Our Past*. Milwaukee: Gareth Stevens, 2002.

McIntosh, Jane. *Archaeology*. New York: Dorling Kindersley, 1998.

Orna-Ornstein, John. *Archaeology: Discovering the Past*. New York: Oxford University Press, 2002.

INDEX

Web Sites

Due to the changing nature of Internet links, the Rosen Publishing Group, Inc., has developed an online list of Web sites related to the subject of this book. This site is updated regularly. Please use this link to access the list:

http://www.rosenlinks.com/gd/ancient/